**Deliberate Plan© for your business.**

**Your guide, your compass on difficult times.**

By: Lisandra Pagán, PhD.

2017 © All rights reserved Lisandra Pagán, PhD.

## Deliberate Plan© for your Business

Did you know that after a disaster 1 of 4 small businesses is forced to close? That never reopens? In fact, according to FEMA and the Small Business Administration 40% of small businesses fail after an interruption. Does your business plan include preparing for the unexpected? Research concludes that those numbers can be decreased if business owners take actions to prepare for disasters.

If your business plan does not include contingency planning, there are many things that you as business owner can do to protect your business and ensure that your business is operating again in a short time following an interruption. I invite you to learn more about the Deliberate Plan©.

My name is Lisandra Pagán, PhD. I am the founder of Deliberate Plan Consulting LLC., and the author and creator of the Deliberate Plan©. I want to help business owners, just like you to prepare for disasters and recover as soon as possible from unexpected disruptions. After brainstorming and researching on ways to create stronger and resilient small businesses I created the Deliberate Plan©.

I believe passionately on helping business owners and individuals to help themselves; empowering them to use the new acquired knowledge and process to take control of unexpected circumstances. It is my goal to help as many business owners as possible to learn more about preparedness and have a prepared, strong and resilient business.

Now, let me advise that this book is not like other books on planning. This book was designed as a workbook, with lines and blank spaces so you can write down your thoughts and take action as you go through the book. What a great idea! Right? You don't have to wait until you read the book to take action, you can start right away.

I have included on this book, all the information I wish someone would have given me before I was forced to close my business, when I thought that a Business Plan was enough.

Also, as added value, I want to offer a complementary Planning session, I made available to users of the Deliberate Plan system. If you want to take advantage of the complementary Planning session before you start creating or while creating your Deliberate Plan, please schedule your call here: http://bit.ly/2nEBk3q

Introduction

The main objective of the Deliberate Plan© is to prepare your business for potential situations that might arise as result of natural or manmade events. In order to develop a plan that takes into consideration the vast majority of risks faced by your business, a rigorous assessment of the business is required. The rigorous assessment will help you determine: Which are the mayor risk for your business? Which are minor risks? Only you, as business owner know what the strong areas of your business are, and which areas are needed to ensure operations at a satisfactory level. That's the reason why your contribution to the planning process is so important. I will provide you guidance, suggestions and recommendations based on my area of expertise. Remember that at the end you will be making decisions to minimize risks in those areas you deem more important. You will also be making the final decisions of which areas of the business you want to protect.

I want to begin by explaining to you, one more time what the Deliberate Plan© is? The Deliberate Plan© is a strategic planning process that provides you as the business owner a practical guide that facilitates the decision making process during times of crisis. It is a strategic planning process, done with the contribution of the business owner, the consultant, and a work team. It is strategic because takes into considerations strengths and weaknesses of the business, its employees, available resources, and contingencies to determine the current state of the business and the final state in which the business owner wants to see the business. Once the Deliberate Plan© is complete it becomes a guide or an instruction manual that facilitates the decision-making process when the unexpected happens or a crisis strikes.

One of the features of the Deliberate Plan is that since it is developed in "peace" times or simply in times when its implementation is not immediately needed, it allows us to see things that otherwise we would have missed. Have you ever looked for something that you know you have seen it recently but you cannot find it? I bet your answer is yes! We all have experienced the frustration of looking for something when you need it the most and not finding it as quickly as you wish. The same situation happens when we try to strategize and to create a rushed plan. When you try to come up with ideas during a crisis it is more difficult or impossible, not to mention that sometimes there will be no time for planning or strategizing. That's why we develop a plan in times when we don't need it immediately. To be able to see things, and find strategies and ideas that under other circumstance we would have missed.

When you don't need to implement the plan immediately, you have time to develop, practice, assess, correct areas that show deficiencies and at the end to have a plan as close to perfect as it will ever be. As result, it flows naturally. The implementation will not necessarily be 100% perfect or as planned but avoids the crisis within the crisis. It also prevents failures in decision making, waste of time, resources and efforts. Now that we understand the importance of the Deliberate Plan, why we plan for contingencies, and the logic of planning ahead, let's get to work!

## Overall Procedure for the Deliberate Plan

1. Conduct a rigorous assessment of the actual state of the business.
2. Identify possible risks, threats, and vulnerabilities of your business (consider the present and the future).
3. For each identified risk, threat and vulnerability assign a number in terms of importance or priority.
4. Develop possible solutions for each risk, threat or vulnerability that you deemed a priority. Select at least two possible solutions.
5. Select the best solution.
6. Develop a plan of action. How would you implement each of the selected solutions? Explain and document your plan.

7. Make the plan available for everyone. Discuss the plan with group leaders and employees.
8. Practice the plan and evaluate the results.
9. Make corrections and improvements when needed.
10. Practice the plan until you are satisfied with the results.

*Step 1: Conduct a rigorous assessment of the actual state of the business.*

A rigorous assessment of the business requires the business owner to answer the question to best of his/her abilities and with complete honesty. You need to understand that this is the first step to preparedness, securing you're the future of your business y possibly doubling your revenues during times of crisis.

The first thing to assess is your contingency plan.

Do you have a contingency plan?

_____

If you have a plan, when was it revised?

_____

Have you discussed your plan with your staff?

_____

Does your staff know that plan exist?

_____

What was the result of the last evaluation?

_____

_____

_____

_____

_____

Does that plan meet the needs of the business?

_____

_____

_____

_____

_____

If you were to implement the plan today, would you be confident the plan will meet the expectations?

_____

_____

_____

_____

_____

If you have never had a plan:

What are the risks your business faces? Think about technology, location, suppliers, supplies you will need and what would happen if you don't have it or have access to them?

_____

_____

_____

_____

_____

_____

_____

What are the things that could stop you from conducting business as usual?

_____

_____

_____

_____

_____

What are the things that could force you to close your business? (Temporarily or permanently)

_____

_____

_____

_____

_____

_____

_____

_____

In case of an emergency, will your employees know what to do?

_____

Have you given your employees a set of instructions on how to proceed in case of emergency?

_____

_____

_____

_____

_____

Have you discussed with your family and employees what will happen to the business if you die? Do they know who to go to? Who would make decisions in your absence?

_____

_____

_____

_____

_____

_____

_____

_____

In the event of an emergency, do your employees know how to determine the steps to follow? Do they know which factors will trigger the activation of an emergency plan and which don't require the activation of the plan?

_____

_____

_____

_____

_____

_____

Do your employees know their role and functions if the emergency plan is activated? Have you trained them on the implementation of the emergency plan?

_____

_____

_____

_____

_____

Have you identified leaders within your employees that could potentially take charge during the implementation of the emergency plan? Have you trained them? Do they know their roles and responsibilities?

_____

_____

_____

_____

_____

_____

_____

After answering these questions to the best of your knowledge and with complete honestly, you most likely have a pretty clear of the current state of preparedness of your business. Use this area to take notes, reflect on the state of preparedness. Write down the current state and the state that you want to achieve.

_____

_____

_____

_____

_____

Current state

_____

_____

_____

_____

_____

_____

_____

End state (what I want to achieve)

_____

_____

_____

_____

_____

_____

_____

Why do you want to achieve it?

_____

_____

_____

_____

_____

_____

_____

***Step 2***: *Identify possible risks, threats, and vulnerabilities of your business (consider the present and the future).*

In step 1, you briefly reviewed which are the possible risks, threats, and vulnerabilities of your business. Let's develop this topic.

Do your business and its operations depend on the use of technology?

_____

_____

_____

Do you have a backup system?

_____

_____

What would happen if your system is hacked?

_____

_____

_____

What if you accidentally delete or lose important information such as financial records, important contacts, legal documents, intellectual property, private information from your customers or employees?

_____

_____

_____

_____

_____

In order to run your business, do you need electrical power or potable water?

_____

_____

_____

_____

How long can your business go without electrical power and potable water?

_____

_____

_____

_____

What would you do if you if there are interruptions in services for a longer period that what your business can go without services?

_____

_____

_____

_____

_____

Could you continue business operations?

Would you have to cease operations or close the business for a period of time?

What would happen to your inventory?

_____

_____

_____

_____

_____

What would happen to your materials, ingredients, resources if there are no services for a long time? Would you lose them? (Think about mold, expiration or use by dates, damaged, refrigeration, etc)

_____

_____

_____

_____

_____

Who depends on your services? How this group would be affected?

_____

_____

_____

_____

_____

What would happen if you cannot continue on business?

_____

_____

_____

_____

_____

Is your business located in a flood, hurricane, tornado, or wild fire prone area? What about civil disruptions, sabotage?

_____

_____

_____

_____

_____

Is the structure where your business resides safe, structurally sound? Does it shows any signs of decay?

_____

_____

_____

_____

_____

_____

_____

Is your business located close to a nuclear plan? Close to any kind of facilities or businesses that can cause harm to people or environmental health?

_____

_____

_____

_____

_____

_____

Is it possible for services or products provided by your business to compromise or harm employees' or customers' health? What about the environment?

Is your business' waste harmful for customers, employees or the environment?

Do you use chemicals or harmful products during operations? Are these required for operations?

_____

_____

_____

_____

_____


Do you have a binder with all Material Safety Data Sheets or MSDS?

_____

_____

_____

_____

_____

Do employees know what MSDS are for? DO they know where to find them?

_____

_____

_____

_____


Is your business located near to a business that manages chemicals as part of their day to day operations?

_____

_____

_____

_____

_____

Do you know if the closest business has an emergency plan?

_____

_____

_____

_____

_____

Do you understand the closest business has high risk operations?

_____

_____

_____

_____

_____

_____

***Step 3****: For each identified risk, threat and vulnerability assign a number in terms of importance or priority.*

Now that you understand the risks associated with your business, operations, neighborhood, and other; let's prioritize!

Which are the biggest risks for your business? Which of the risks concern you the most? Why?

_____

_____

_____

_____

_____

_____

_____

What are minor risks for your business? Why?

What are the potential solutions to minimize your risks? How would you minimize the risks of your business?

_____

_____

_____

_____

What are the potential strategies? What methods would you use?

_____

_____

_____

_____

_____

_____

_____

_____

_____

_____

_____

_____

_____

_____

_____

_____

From the list of solutions and strategies; which ones are the most realistic and achievable? (Please consider time, effort, resources, personnel, and finances).

_____

_____

_____

_____

Which of the realist and achievable strategies would you implement first? What is your priority?

_____

_____

Which strategies would you implement at a later time?

Which ones are not priorities? Why are not priorities?

_____

_____

_____

_____

_____

_____

_____

_____

_____

_____

Which risks are not important at all to you, or are you willing to take a chance on them and not do anything about it?

Why are you willing to take that chance?

***Step 4***: *Develop possible solutions for each risk, threat or vulnerability that you deemed a priority. Select at least two possible solutions.*

Now to the meaty gritty!

Possible solutions for the risks you deemed a priority, those which really concern you.

_____

_____

_____

_____

_____

_____

_____

_____

Select the best two options for each risk:

*The best solutions are solutions that we can implement. Be realistic and don't choose solutions that you will not be able to implement or are too complicated:*

_____

_____

_____

_____

_____

_____

_____

_____

_____

_____

_____

_____

_____

_____

_____

_____

_____

Compare your options and select the best option. (Which ones are realistic and attainable? Why is one better than the other? Do you have the resources? What is the required level of effort for each? Am I willing and available to implement the option?)

_____

_____

_____

_____

_____

_____

_____

_____

_____

Continue to Compare your options and select the best option.

_____

_____

_____

_____

_____

_____

_____

_____

_____

***Step 5***: *Select the best solution.*

What are my solutions? Are these solutions going to help me achieve the end state I want for my business? Reflect on your selection.

_____

_____

_____

_____

_____

_____

_____

_____

_____

_____

_____

Best solutions:

_____

_____

_____

_____

_____

_____

_____

Realistic solutions:

_____

_____

_____

_____

_____

_____

Do you have doubts, or concerns? Does anything still worry you? Write it down!

_____

_____
_____
_____
_____
_____
_____
_____
_____
_____

***Step 6***: *Develop a plan of action. How would you implement each of the selected solutions? Explain and document your plan.*

Select a RED Team. Your RED team is a group of people that have shown you leadership skills and that understand your business as you do. The RED team will help you in the implementation of your Deliberate Plan. Discuss with your RED team the strategies that you have selected and let them help you determine who will be fit to each role. This is a critical step for the development of the plan. First, you and your RED team know and understand the business and its operations. Your Red team and you as the owner know your employees and probably have identified potential players. During this process you and your RED team will strategize in terms of operations and implementation. The consultant will provide guidance in terms of decision making.

Your strategies and operations must be documented step by step. The final document must include detail so that the RED team or the business personnel could implement the plan or "call the plan" without needing the authorization or guidance of the business owner. It is necessary to include which are the situations that trigger "calling the plan" and which do not. For example:

> *Juan is the RED team leader; he walks into the business lobby and witnessed a customer collapsing in what looks like a life or death situation. Juan immediately knows what to do. He realizes he doesn't need to "call the plan" but to call 9-1-1. Juan grabs the phone and calls 9-1-1, removes other customers from the area, and assigns another team member to stay with the customer while medical assistance arrives. Since this event happened in the lobby, immediate operations are delayed while the*

> *situation is under control. After contacting 9-1-1 and having a medical team on its way, Juan contacts the business owner.*

This scenario describes how Juan knew the logical, rehearsed order of actions. It also describes how Juan was not paralyzed by fear and knew exactly what to do. He knew the situation did not require to "call the plan" but instead:

1. Assess the emergency.
2. Call 9-1-1.
3. Remove customers and other personnel from the scene so there is room to assist the person in need.
4. Delay operations including ignoring phones, orders, etc. until the situation is under control.
5. Contact the owner once help is on its way.

Let's review Juan's scenario. Can you imagine what could have gone wrong if Juan didn't know what to do? He probably would have called the owner to ask what to do. Maybe business operations would have continued while some customer tried to contact 9-1-1? What would have happened if Juan has gotten paralyzed by fear? All of these situations are possible responses. Every human is different and we all have different ways to react. This is why it is extremely necessary to document a detailed plan, to communicate it and to make it available to everyone as a reference.

In contrast, if that same scenario would have included a second person collapsing, Juan's response would have been completely different. Juan would have had to "call the plan". He would have had to implement the **Deliberate Plan**. The plan would have probably included calling local authorities and launching an investigation. In that case, Juan wouldn't have been able to remove anything or anyone from the scene. Instead he would have had to find an alternate area to hold people and count witnesses, and so on. This is why I make emphasis on having a **Deliberate Plan** which is not a cookie cutter but a customized plan.

Since not all the time your RED team will have to "call the plan", you will also need to develop a list of "triggers". Triggers are situations that require the implementation of the plan or "calling the plan". The list must also include scenarios in which "calling the plan" is not necessary. The Deliberate Plan is scalable which means it can be "called" as needed. Sometimes you will have an event that will not require its implementation but as the situation evolves you might have to "call it". In contrast, there will also be some events that require the implementation but as the event evolves it can be managed in a smaller scale. As such, the plan can be "called back" or "recalled", which is nothing but a cancellation of the implementation.

\*\* **At this stage you need to develop a detailed implementation plan. Describe in details the steps to take when "calling the plan". Establish from the beginning the "triggers" and make a list of the events that are NOT "triggers".**

The first page of your final document must include the list of "triggers". I recommend that you make extra copies of the first page and place them everywhere! In the break room, bathroom, stairs, everywhere they can read it. It is critical that your employees and team leaders know if possible what situations are "triggers" and which are not. If they cannot memorize them, then you need to have copies available. It is always a possibility that someone may call the plan without needing it, that's something you can address at a later time. However, if the plan is needed and it's not "called" the consequences can be fatal. So please, remind them what requires implementation and what does not. I personally believe it is better to "call it" and don't need it, than not calling it and regretting the decision. So be nice, if sometime is called without a real need. Use the opportunity as a learning experience and as a reminder that additional training is needed.

_____

_____

_____

_____

_____

***Step 7****: Make the plan available for everyone. Discuss the plan with group leaders and employees.*

All the time, money, and effort you have invested in the Deliberate Plan is going to be worthless if you do not communicate the plan. If you do not communicate the plan it will end up being another binder, another manual, or folder collecting dust somewhere (if it doesn't end in the trash). Make copies of the plan, give a copy to your leaders so they can read it and have it as reference. Make extra copies just in case someone picks up interest and wants to read it (sometimes vendors spend a lot of time in your office, it will be perfect if they learn about the plan just in case they are there when something happens). Better than paper copies, have it as a PDF and email it to your leaders and employees. That does not mean that they will read it, but at least they will know where it is when they need it. Don't keep your copy in your desk, have a digital copy on your smart phone, have a copy on your car. You never know when you are going to need it.

Discuss the plan. Spend some time discussing the plan with your staff. Do NOT assume they will read it, discuss it in details and have a questions and answers section if needed. The Deliberate Plan is another fruit of your effort, time, and dedication be proud of it! Delegate responsibilities and create an incentive program if it's needed. If your employees get involved you can train them and have additional RED team members. The idea is to get the excited about the plan and avoiding that they see it as another thing to do. After all, the implementation depends on everyone! So does their job and the future of the business.

***Step 8****: Practice the plan and evaluate the results.*

Practice makes perfect! The plan will work as a system when all its components work in alignment. That's why it is so important to train employees, and teach them the importance of their participation for the success of the team. No one will be able to pull the plan alone! This is team effort. So, practice the plan. Start by doing something small. For example: practice how would you keep the business running for three days without electricity. Let them learn, make mistakes, it is just a practice. Don't get frustrated. There will always be mistakes. You will always discover who are the stronger players and who are not good handling stressful situations, but that's also a gain.

You will be able to see what works and what doesn't. You will have clearer picture on how to assign teams, who have leadership skills, and who simply cannot work under pressure. The practice will also give you the opportunity to evaluate strategies. Evaluate the results of the practice and address those areas of need. Isn't it awesome that you are not on a real crisis and that you can correct what didn't work? Re-assign, move people around, changes roles and responsibilities if it's necessary! This is the perfect time to see who cannot handle the pressure!

Thoughts/ concerns:

_____

_____

_____

Thoughts / Concerns:

***Step 9****: Make corrections and improvements when needed.*

If you are like me, I am never satisfied with my Christmas tree. Every single day of the Christmas season I move ornaments around. No, I'm not OCD (obsessive compulsive disorder) but I am never satisfied. During the day, I move ornaments because I can see empty areas, and during the night when the lights are on, I see how the ornaments block the little lights. This should be your approach. The **Deliberate Plan** is a living document, which means that needs to be reviewed frequently. It needs to be examined because employees come and go. It needs to be reviewed to see when the ornaments block the lights, or someone impedes the success of the plan. Also when there are empty areas, or too many ornaments (people) in one place. Don't forget that people will leave without notice or giving you time to find another leader for the RED team, that's why succession planning is important and continued training so new leaders can emerge.

At the same time, you will find that while some people might pick up interest and would want to be part of the RED team, there will be others that will give up the task in a heartbeat. Identify potential RED team members from day one, work with them and train them without making too much noise. Remember consequences can be fatal if someone panics, freezes and it's unable to act. Practice and move your players if needed. Your RED team is your support, so make sure you build a strong one.

In terms of training I recommend a monthly session at least during the first couple of months. It is important that employees and leaders understand the Deliberate Plan and know what each term means. Once your team understands implementation, they become more involved and will provide ideas and suggestions on how to improve the plan or training. When everything is going well, you can reduce trainings to once every three months and a brief meeting a month. Practice diverse scenarios and delegate training to team members. Remember they need to know what to do when you are not around, so don't be limited to training when you are available. Have training in different shifts, with or without you. Evaluate once every six months and witness the improvement. Keep them interested and motivated, you will develop a strong, well trained team.

Thoughts/ Concerns:

_____

_____

_____

_____

_____

_____

_____

_____

_____

***Step 10****: Practice the plan until you are satisfied with the results.*

Just like I mentioned on Step 9, the Deliberate Plan is a living document, you never will be 100% satisfied. There will always be someone who needs additional training, or someone who leaves and leaves a leadership position within the RED team. There will always be some evolving risks; as such new revisions are needed. That is the whole purpose of a living document, that you cannot be complacent! It is the opposite; the Deliberate Plan will push you to prepare. So when I say, practice the plan until you are satisfied; it means practice, practice, practice.

Research has shown that those who become complacent and settle; when they need to act, they find out they were not as prepared as they thought. I invite you to assess your business and its risks at least once a year. Evaluate trends and preferences of customers. I also invite you to avoid complacency, to avoid putting the plan in a drawer or let it collect dust. Take it out for a spin once in a while. Adapt it to the evolving reality of this century's businesses. Your **Deliberate Plan** was developed to help your business. Remember your business is your patrimony, your legacy, don't let it to chance.

It is my desire that you find the peace that comes by knowing that you have done everything that was in your hands. I wish you the best for you and your business, I want to see you succeed. If you ever find yourself concerned about your plan, contact me I can help. Visit my website http://deliberateplan.com

But before we part ways, I want to remind you that, you could book a complementary Planning session with me here:

http://bit.ly/2nEBk3q

I recommend you go through the material so we can address doubts or concerns during the Planning session. However, if you find yourself confused at some point or need clarification, please visit my website www.deliberateplan.com and submit your questions. I will answer them.

You will also find free resources, tools, and additional worksheets on my website. I also offer virtual workshops and webinars. Sign up to receive invites to my virtual workshops! For those interested I offer one on one consulting. Just get in touch and we will find a way to tailor a plan that fits the needs of your business! It is my wish that every business owner give his/her business the opportunity to recover from challenges or setbacks. It is my pleasure to help business owners like you! God bless you and your business.

www.ingramcontent.com/pod-product-compliance
Lightning Source LLC
Chambersburg PA
CBHW061445180526
45170CB00004B/1564